CONTENTS

1

INTRODUCTION

"Look at the birds of the air, for they neither sow nor reap nor gather into barns; yet your heavenly Father feeds them. Are you not of more value than they?" - Matthew 6:26

Much can be learned from the birds that welcome the dawn with singing and bid farewell to the dusk with the same melody. Do they not sense danger? Do they not experience privation and hardship? From where does their peace and joy arise? Surely not from the absence of danger.

A bald eagle, for example, can spot its prey between three to four miles away and plan its deadly attack. How can the little birds, who for certain know that they have enemies out there, still sing their melodious songs?

When the hummingbird or the sparrow flutter about among the flowers of the field, it seems that they are absolutely carefree. Though danger is present all around them, there is peace in knowing that their next meal of nectar or seed is readily available, and their nest high in the trees will keep them sheltered. It's almost absurd to imagine these tiny creatures fretting over where their next paycheck is coming from or how they will pay their bills.

The power that allows the birds to take flight is the same power that keeps them soaring in the air through the tempest, feeds them in moments of privation, and keeps them safe in the presence of their enemies. Our Heavenly Father reveals His care for us in that selfsame way, especially when the storms of life threaten to steal our joy. The journey toward lasting peace and happiness is often unclear; however, Jesus Christ provides the answer. In this book, we explore ten key principles that lead the way to true happiness. The following chapters explore:

1. Gratitude for Greater You: The power of expressing gratitude is recognized not only throughout the Holy Scriptures but also in acade-

mia. Through gratitude, we connect to God in a new and vibrant way.

2. Dedicate Your Life Entirely To God: Surrendering our will to God will lead to difficult decisions, but those who commit to Christ will be honored by Him.

3. Make Your Goal in Accordance With God's Will: True fulfillment comes from seeking to align our dreams and aspirations as closely to God's goals for us as possible.

4. Do Not Let His Word Depart from You: While many seek after the wisdom of this world, it is only in the Bible that we can find guidance and solace amidst life's storms.

5. Be Humble: Reflecting the character of Christ in humility is a sacred call for every believer.

6. Always Sow What You Want to Reap: Every seed that we sow will produce a corresponding harvest, a principle that applies to all areas of life.

7. Be Persistent In Everything You Do: In the face of adversity, we can persevere in the Lord's strength. When human effort unites with divine power, the heights we can reach are unimaginable.

8. Let God Guide You: Trusting in God alone, we can be strengthened through all of life's greatest challenges.

9. Do Not Accomplish Things in a Sinful Way: Integrity and righteousness pave the path to lasting joy. We should rest in the Lord and leave the consequences of difficult situations to Him.

10. Be Obedient to Authorities: Throughout the Bible, we are given countless appeals to respect the authorities set up by God, for in this, we honor God Himself.

Dear Friend, as you read this book, may Jesus Christ reveal Himself to you as your constant friend, caring Savior, and source of everlasting joy. Know that just as He watches over each little sparrow, Our God watches over you.

GRATITUDE FOR A GREATER YOU

At 3:00 AM, the aggressive rocking of the crib and Johnny's screaming shattered the silence of the night. Deep in slumber, Mommy awoke to the urgent plea of her 1-year-old son. Rushing to him, Rachel discovered that Johnny's only demand was hunger. Despite the lack of gratitude in his cries, it was evident that he lacked the ability to express himself differently. At such a tender age, Johnny's behavior was considered excusable, as he was too young and immature to communicate his needs in a more pleasant manner.

Are your personal behaviors excusable? Today, some authors and scholars argue that the absence of gratitude is a sign of immaturity, prompting us to wonder how many individuals, like Johnny, have physically grown up without learning the power and importance of gratitude. This suggests a physical development without corresponding emotional growth. However, one might question the significance of gratitude and whether it is truly essential.

Countless scientific articles have demonstrated a direct link between gratitude and one's optimal health. "Expressing gratitude," one author from the American Heart Association indicated, "can improve sleep, mood, and immunity, and can decrease depression, anxiety, chronic pain, and disease."[1] In addition, Michael E. McCullough, from the University of Miami, has researched extensively on the topic of gratitude. In one study, McCullough, along with his team, requested that the participants jot down a few thoughts focusing on a certain topic.

66 One group wrote about things they were grateful for that had occurred during the week. A second group wrote about daily irritations or things that had displeased them, and the third wrote about events that had affected them (with no emphasis on them being

positive or negative). After 10 weeks, those who wrote about gratitude were more optimistic and felt better about their lives. Surprisingly, they also exercised more and had fewer visits to physicians than those who focused on sources of aggravation.[2]

Furthermore, renowned figures in leadership, such as Napoleon Hill, have emphasized the intrinsic connection between success and health. "No person," in his own words, "may enjoy outstanding success without good health." Gratitude leads to good health, which in turn aids with your success. Therefore, if you want to be great, begin by being grateful; greatness is preceded by gratefulness. Seeking greatness without gratefulness is much like planning a journey without a horse to pull the carriage.

Historical-ecclesiastical leaders, whose shoulders modern theologians stand upon today, were known for their gratitude. Consider the life of the Apostle Paul, for instance, who authored significant works from prison, addressing "some of the most liberating concepts imaginable."[3]

The cold winter of the Roman cell proved impotent and incapable of extinguishing the warmth of Paul's faith and courage. In the deep abyss of that dark prison, with a positive mood and mindset, he offered the world a glimpse into his illuminated heart. Dipping the pen of his courage into the ink of joy, he proclaimed to the world: "Rejoice in the Lord always: and again I say, Rejoice" (Philippians 4:4).

Paul was far from being a despondent prisoner. Even from his confinement, he reassured the Ephesians: I "Cease not to give thanks for you, making mention of you in my prayers." Additionally, to the Colossians, he expressed gratitude, saying: "We give thanks to God and the Father of our Lord Jesus Christ, praying always for you" (Ephesians 1:16; Colossians 1:3).

Given that gratitude is a universally accessible power, how can we start practicing it today?

An article from Harvard suggests the following:

1) **"Write a thank-you note.** You can make yourself happier and nurture your relationship with another person by <u>writing a thank-you letter</u> or email expressing your enjoyment and appreciation

of that person's impact on your life. Send it, or better yet, deliver and read it in person if possible. Make a habit of sending at least one gratitude letter a month. Once in a while, write one to yourself.

2) Thank someone mentally. No time to write? It may help just to think about someone who has done something nice for you, and mentally thank the individual.

3) Keep a gratitude journal. Make it a habit to write down or share with a loved one thoughts about the gifts you've received each day.

4) Count your blessings. Pick a time every week to sit down and write about your blessings — reflecting on what went right or what you are grateful for. Sometimes it helps to pick a number — such as three to five things — that you will identify each week. As you write, be specific and think about the sensations you felt when something good happened to you.

5) Pray. People who are religious can use prayer to cultivate gratitude."[4]

We sincerely desire to see you healthy and happier. Therefore, we prioritize reminding you of the Lord's principle for a satisfying life. To start practicing gratefulness through journaling, as recommended by Harvard, *you may start with simply journaling for 15 to 20 minutes per day. Blessings.*

---

1. "Thankfulness: How Gratitude Can Help Your Health," www.heart.org, n.d., https://www.heart.org/en/healthy-living/healthy-lifestyle/mental-health-and-wellbeing/thankfulness-how-gratitude-can-help-your-health#:~:text=Research%20has%20shown%20that%20that.
2. "Giving Thanks Can Make You Happier," Harvard Health, August 14, 2021, https://www.health.harvard.edu/health beat/giving-thanks-can-make-you-happier.
3. "The Prison Epistles," Alphacrucis College, n.d., https://www.ac.edu.au/units/bib252-the-prison-epistles/#:~:text=Details%20for%20The%20Prison%20Epistles.
4. "Giving Thanks Can Make You Happier," Harvard Health, August 14, 2021, https://www.health.harvard.edu/health beat/giving-thanks-can-make-you-happier.

3
———

DEDICATE YOUR LIFE ENTIRELY TO GOD

I n the summer of 1950, Jim Elliot embarked on a significant journey. Having recently graduated from Wheaton College in Illinois with a focus on linguistics, he set out to spread the gospel by translating the Bible into various native languages in South America. Elliot had been a passionate, devoted, and strong man of God for many years, and he was ready for the next challenge ahead. Later, accompanied by his wife Elisabeth, Elliot boarded a ship from California to Ecuador, not knowing that it was the very last time that he would see his home and immediate family.

Joined by several other missionary families, Elliot and his companions turned their attention to an unreached tribe deep in the Ecuadorian jungle. His greatest desire was that his life and legacy would honor God and that he would be used to win many souls into the everlasting kingdom. For months, the missionaries fervently prayed for the Auca tribe, sending peace offerings and diligently studying their language in hopes of making a connection. Finally, on January 8, 1956, the five men of the group, Jim Elliot, Pete Fleming, Nate Saint, Eddy McCulley, and Roger Youderain landed at the bank of the Curaray River near the Auca camp. Tragically, within hours, the Christian missionaries were discovered speared to death.

Jim Elliot had dedicated his life to spreading the gospel, and as a young man, ended up losing it for that same cause. While this reality might be discouraging to some, Matthew 16 provides hope for the Christian who wants to entirely dedicate their life to God:

66 Then said Jesus unto his disciples, If any man will come after me, let him deny himself, and take up his cross, and follow me. **For whosoever will save his life shall lose it: and whosoever will lose his life for my sake shall find it.** For what is a man profited, if he shall gain the whole world, and lose his own

soul? or what shall a man give in exchange for his soul?

— MATTHEW 16:24-26

In these verses, Jesus addresses His disciples, anticipating the challenging times ahead as they embark on their ministries without His physical presence. He foresees the intense persecution they will endure. Jesus emphasizes the importance of prioritizing eternal significance over temporary gains, warning against investing in endeavors devoid of lasting impact. He urges bravery in surrendering one's life to Him, regardless of the sacrifices it may entail, affirming that such devotion is the path to true success, a sense of fulfillment and purpose.

Several years later, after mourning the tragic deaths of their husbands, Elisabeth Elliot and Rachel Saint demonstrated remarkable courage and faith by returning to Ecuador to continue their mission work with the Auca tribe. The love and forgiveness of Christ enabled them to persevere in fulfilling the Great Commission to "make disciples of all nations." Over time, they were able to establish peaceful contact with the Aucas and bring them the Gospel. Within a matter of months, the violent tribe that speared their husbands to death invited the missionary wives to live and share the Bible with them in their own language. Finally, their hearts were won to the Lord. Though the conversion of the natives came at a great cost it still holds true that "He is no fool who gives what he cannot keep to gain what he cannot lose."[1]

What are you willing to give up? Dedication to God often doesn't necessitate physical sacrifice, as in the case of Jim Elliot and the other missionaries who paid the ultimate price. Yet, for the missionary wives like Elisabeth Elliot and Rachel Saint, it meant surrendering bitterness and hatred towards the Aucas. Their act of forgiveness and ongoing efforts to reconcile with the tribe exemplified their total commitment.

When we dedicate our lives to God, it's about entrusting our future to Him and inviting His presence to guide us. It entails relinquishing control and embracing His will, even when it requires forgiving those who have wronged us and persisting in difficult circumstances. Our prayers in such times should ever be:

Father, lead me day by day,

Ever in Thine own good way;
Teach me to be pure and true,
Show me what I ought to do.

When in danger, make me brave;
Make me know that Thou canst save;
Keep me safely by Thy side;
Let me in Thy love abide.

When I'm tempted to do wrong,
Make me steadfast, wise, and strong;
And when all alone I stand,
Shield me with Thy mighty hand.

May I do the good I know,
Serving gladly here below;
Then at last go home to Thee,
Evermore Thine own to be.[2]

Dear Friend, It's often the small, everyday choices that reveal our willingness to submit to God's guidance towards true success. When we consistently honor Him in the little things, we'll find the strength to remain faithful even in the face of great challenges. By inviting Him into our hearts, we allow Him to shape our motives, thoughts, and decisions.

May you find the courage to surrender every aspect of your life to God, knowing that He will faithfully guide you through every step of your journey.

Warm regards.

---

1. Staff, "About Jim Elliot · Elisabeth Elliot," https://elisabethelliot.org/, n.d., https://elisabethelliot.org/about/jim-elliot/.

2. "Father, Lead Me Day by Day," Hymnary.org, accessed March 25, 2024, https://hymnary.org/text/father_lead_me_day_by_day.

4

MAKE YOUR GOAL IN
ACCORDANCE WITH GOD'S WILL

D o you follow your heart as a god in whom you believe, or do you believe in a God whom your heart needs to follow? The answer to this question might, in my opinion, be the greatest determinant as to whether one is a Christian or not.

While Satan works through the atheistic community, continually at war against Christianity from without, he is by no means avoiding the strategy of creating issues from within Christianity. Although atheism may be a blunt way of rejecting God, it isn't worse than any ideology that seeks to deify humanity and divert the minds of the masses from the true God, all while claiming to be Christian.

How do we do this? By telling the world that there is a god within them. If this is the case, then why do I need Jesus Christ? If the very essence of God resides within me, then rather than seeking Jesus externally, I can find answers to difficult questions and solutions to problems by searching within myself.

However, I am afraid that if left alone, fallen human nature is nothing better than a helpless babe in a lonely crib. What can they do but cry for aid? When they dirty their diaper, they can't even clean themselves. When they grow hungry, they can't feed themselves. If there be, therefore, any lesson from a helpless babe in a crib, it is parental dependence. After all, we are called "children of God" (1 John 3:1).

Given that, naturally, we are as helpless children, we ought to always seek help and direction from "our Father which is in heaven" (Matthew 6:9). He is the eternal and almighty One who declared: "I am God, and there is no one like Me, declaring the end from the beginning, And from ancient times things which have not been done, Saying, 'My plan will be established, And I will accomplish all My good pleasure'" (Isaiah 46:9, 10).

On the other hand, as a fallen human being, my "heart is deceitful above all things, and desperately wicked: who can know it?" (Jeremiah 17:9). Furthermore, all "things which proceed out of the mouth come forth from the heart; and they defile the man" (Matthew 15:18-19).

There is indeed an astounding contrast between the religion of Jesus Christ and the new age spirituality that tells us to find God within us. When I look within, all I see is that "out of the heart proceed evil thoughts, murders, adulteries, fornications, thefts, false witness, blasphemies" (Matthew 15:19).

With this thought in mind, one of the greatest missionaries during the existence of nazism – Corrie Ten Boom – said it best: "If you look at the world, you'll be distressed. If you look within, you'll be depressed. If you look at God, you'll be at rest."[1]

Apparently brethren, "Following our hearts" is the heart of our problems. But "all who are being led by the Spirit of God, these are sons and daughters of God" (Romans 8:14). To say it differently, let's borrow from the wise words of Ravi Zacharias.

66 "If God is the author of life, there must be a script. Where there is a script, there must be a story. It is not that the

world is a stage and we can pick and choose different scripts. The individual subplot must gain its direction from the larger story of God's purpose for our lives."[2]

We conclude, therefore, that the most prudent course of action is to align our plans and aspirations with the divine will of God, entrusting Him with the guidance of our lives. "Many are the plans in a person's heart," Solomon once wrote, "but it is the Lord's purpose that prevails" (Proverbs 19:21). Goals without God are like a night sky without stars, lacking in beauty or engineless cars, lacking in purpose. May God's unfailing providence lead you on your path.

Blessings.

---

1. "A Quote by Corrie Ten Boom," www.goodreads.com, n.d., https://www.goodreads.com/quotes/32394-if-you-look-at-the-world-you-ll-be-distressed-if.
2. Ravi Zacharias at Christ Church Presbyterian, Atlanta, June 21, 2016

5

DO NOT LET HIS WORD DEPART FROM YOU

L ife is a bullet train. If you blink twice, you might miss a century. But do not get off at the station of lamentation yet. The ebbing hours and flowing days of a man are perhaps his best blessing. Therefore, it matters how you perceive yourself. The day you become convinced that you will forever possess the elastic and smooth skin of a child, the muscles of an athlete, and various abilities you may now have, you will have performed the greatest self-harm possible.

It is when we understand that we are both frail and finite that we will do all in our power to rise to the height of the clouds, even if that means exposing ourselves to high winds. When we understand that beauty is a fading flower with a limited lifespan, we become great stewards of it, building relationships on the concrete foundation of character. When we realize we were given a 100% battery-life with no charger, we stop the unnecessary browsing of this world, close vain tabs, and visit the sites that matter most for the now and eternity.

You may search heaven and earth, high mountains and dark caverns, hills and valleys, and you will not find a wiser counsel than the one handed down from the family of King David. "So teach us," he requested, "to number our days, that we may apply our hearts unto wisdom" (Psalm 90:12). Furthermore, Solomon built on his father's knowledge when he declared, "It is better to go to the house of mourning than to go to the house of feasting, for that is the end of all men, and the living will lay it to his heart" (Ecclesiastes 7:2).

Nonetheless, feasting isn't inherently sinful. In the book of Luke (refer to Luke 15), Jesus shared three parables emphasizing the importance of celebrating at fitting moments. However, the current world tempts us with feasts so frequent and varied that they almost seem designed to dull our senses, steering us away from the wisdom provided by Joshua's counsel: "Keep this Book of the Law always on your lips; meditate on it day and night, so that you may be careful to do everything written in it. Then you will be prosperous and successful" (Joshua 1:8).

The wisdom that leads to success lies in recognizing that life cannot be a continuous feast. Vacations only find meaning when balanced with earnest work. It's unrealistic to think that our present opportunities will forever be available. Seize the moments, cling to the Word of God, and profess your faith continually.

The renowned British journalist Malcolm Muggeridge did well in painting a vivid picture of a short life when he stated:

> "We look back upon history and what do we see?
>
> Empires rising and falling, revolutions and counterrevolutions, wealth accumulating and and then disbursed, one nation dominant and then another. Shakespeare speaks of the 'rise and fall of great ones that ebb and flow with the moon.'
>
> In one lifetime I have seen my own countrymen ruling over a quarter of the world, the great majority of them

convinced, in the words of what is still a favorite song, that 'God who's made them mighty would make them mightier yet.'

I've heard a crazed, cracked Austrian proclaim to the world the establishment of a German Reich that would last for a thousand years; an Italian clown announce he would restart the calendar to begin with his own assumption of power; a murderous Georgian brigand in the Kremlin acclaimed by the intellectual elite of the western world as wiser than Solomon, more enlightened than Asoka, more humane than Marcus Aurelius.

I've seen America wealthier and in terms of military weaponry more powerful than all the rest of the world put together, so that Americans, had they so wished, could have outdone an Alexander or a Julius Caesar in the range and scale of their conquests.

All in one little lifetime. All gone with the wind.

England now part of an island off the coast of Europe and threatened with dismemberment and even bankruptcy.

Hitler and Mussolini dead and remembered only in infamy.

Stalin a forbidden name in the regime he helped to found and dominate for some three decades.

America haunted by fears of running out of the precious fluid that keeps the motorways roaring and the smog settling, with troubled memories of a disastrous campaign in Vietnam and of the great victories of the Don Quixotes of the media when they charged the windmills of Watergate. All in one lifetime, all in one lifetime, all gone. Gone with the wind."[1]

How could I build on what Muggeridge has already established? I hope you've caught a glimpse of the notion that Life is short. Therefore, live it, love it, keeping God always first. Do not let the word of God depart from you.

Activity: Write down five things you desire to accomplish, choose the easiest one, and start working towards it today. Take even one small step. Once you have the first accomplishment, give thanks to God, call a friend, and celebrate.

#1

#2

#3

#4

#5

.

---

1. —Malcom Muggeridge, "But Not of Christ," *Seeing Through the Eye: Malcolm Muggeridge on Faith*, ed. Cecil Kuhne (San Francisco: Ignatius Press, 2005), 29-30.

6

BE HUMBLE

The Scottish physician who later became a renowned Christian missionary and explorer in Africa once relinquished every bit of comfort he possessed, immersing himself in the turbulent waters of the African mission field. David Livingstone understood the sacrifice of spending months, if not years, away from his family. He knew the profound sensation of acquiring lost souls at the expense of first-world privileges and fleeting pleasures. Above all, Livingstone was adept at humbling himself before God, acknowledging his helplessness.[1]

This giant of a man was a prayer warrior. The one who passed away on his knees knew both how to talk to God and keep a fiery desire for missions and selfless services to others in his heart continually. In one of his prayers, he cried out to the Almighty saying: "If success attend me, grant me humility; If failure, resignation to Thy will."[2]

What an astounding attitude of humility. Many sincere Christians may possess what it takes to organize a great mission, and they may even have a vision that, if carried out, could quench hunger and eradicate poverty. However, the predominant pride in putrefied hearts prevents many from branching out into the world as a fruitful vine for the Lord.

Therefore, dear child of God, live in humility. Live like your Savior Jesus Christ. He walked the "Via-Dolorosa" for you and for me. But the question remains: would you do the same for others? Are you willing to choose the lot of self-abnegation with an endless resolution to always offer yourself on the altar of service for the downtrodden? This requires humility.

Humility is when you seek the welfare of others above your own. Humility is when you purposely lose an argument in order to win a friend. It's when you conceal your extravagant titles in order to fit in a crowd of common people. Humility is when you accept your mistakes and drop your sheet on the desk of God as the instructor, saying: "Master, I have messed up, please help me."

The renown Christian apologist, Ravi Zacharias, often treaded this terrain. He often spoke on the malefic power of pride and the benefit of humility. On this note, he said it best when he cited the following poem.

He came to my desk with a quiv-
    ering lip,
the lesson was done.
"Have you a new sheet for me, dear
    teacher?
I've spoiled this one."
I took his sheet, all soiled and
    blotted
and gave him a new one all
    unspotted.
And into his tired heart I cried,
"Do better now, my child."
I went to the throne with a trem-
    bling heart,
the day was done.
"Have you a new day for me, dear
    Master?
I've spoiled this one."

He took my day, all soiled and
     blotted
and gave me a new one all
     unspotted.
And into my tired heart He cried,
"Do better now, my child."[3]

Precious son and priceless daughter of God, have you any concern as to how you lived yesterday or even yesteryear? God is a compassionate Father. Bring to him your blotted sheet. Bring to him your messed up projects and plans. Bring it all to him. Do not retain anything. This is the beauty of humility! It renders it all at the feet of God singing the good ole hymn:

Lord Jesus, for this I most humbly
     entreat,
I wait, blessed Lord, at Thy cruci-
     fied feet;
By faith, for my cleansing I see Thy
     blood flow,
Now wash me and I shall be whiter
     than snow.

This is the third stanza of the hymn Whiter

Than Snow: sing the complete hymn and worship God for his mercies that endures forever.

> Lord Jesus, I long to be perfectly
>   whole;
> I want Thee forever to live in my
>   soul,
> Break down every idol, cast out
>   every foe;
> Now wash me and I shall be whiter
>   than snow.

Refrain:
Whiter than snow, yes, whiter than
    snow,
Now wash me, and I shall be whiter
    than snow.

> Lord Jesus, look down from Thy
>   throne in the skies,
> And help me to make a complete
>   sacrifice;
> I give up myself, and whatever I
>   know,
> Now wash me and I shall be whiter
>   than snow.

Lord Jesus, for this I most humbly
    entreat,
I wait, blessed Lord, at Thy cruci-
    fied feet;
By faith, for my cleansing I see Thy
    blood flow,
Now wash me and I shall be whiter
    than snow.

Lord Jesus, Thou seest I patiently
    wait,
Come now, and within me a new
    heart create;
To those who have sought Thee,
    Thou never saidst "No,"
Now wash me and I shall be whiter
    than snow.[4]

Lord Jesus, for this, I most humbly entreat, the precious gift of humility. Your sacred word reminds me that you lift "up the humble" and cast "the wicked down to the ground" (Psalm 147:6). I want to be lifted up from the misery of sin to live under Your grace. Lord, I humbly accept the fact that "God resists the proud, but gives grace to the humble" (James 4:6). In Jesus name, AMEN!

1. George Albert Shepperson, "David Livingstone | Biography, Expeditions, & Facts," in *Encyclopædia Britannica*, December 30, 2018, https://www.britannica.com/biography/David-Livingstone.

2. "David Livingstone Quote: 'If Success Attend Me, Grant Me Humility; If Failure, Resignation to Thy Will.,'" quotefancy.com, accessed March 6, 2024, https://quotefancy.com/quote/1300240/David-Livingstone-If-success-attend-me-grant-me-humility-If-failure-resignation-to-Thy.

3. "Ravi Zacharias - Humble," www.youtube.com, September 11, 2011, https://www.youtube.com/watch?v=M5_6EoL_Yqk.

4. "Whiter than Snow," Hymnary.org, accessed March 7, 2024, https://hymnary.org/text/lord_jesus_i_long_to_be_perfectly_whole.

7

ALWAYS SOW WHAT YOU WANT
TO REAP

One of the most known scriptures in the Canon uses two of the most pertinent verbs in the context of our relation to God and to each other. As you probably have already imagined, the two verbs are "to love" and "to give." "For God so loved the world, that He gave His only begotten Son" (John 3:16).

God loved, then He gave. The sequence found in this verse is a lesson in itself. "To love" must precede "to give." For this reason, the relational message of the cross is, "If you love Me, keep My commandments" (John 14:15). We can't render honor and glory through living a life of obedience to a God whom we do not love. Love must always precede giving lest the gift becomes tainted and polluted by ill intentions.

When we sincerely go to God and "love Him, because He first loved us" (1 John 4:19), giving will have finally become a cheerful thing. When we heed the command, "You shall love your neighbor as yourself" (Matthew 22:39), we will also have conquered the bitterness of letting go and present ourselves unto the LORD as cheerful givers.

> "God declares, "Blessed are ye that sow beside all waters." Isaiah 32:20. A continual imparting of God's gifts wherever the cause of God or the needs of humanity demand our aid, does not tend to poverty. "There is that scattereth, and yet increaseth; and there is that withholdeth more than is meet, but it tendeth to poverty." Proverbs 11:24. The sower multiplies his seed by casting it away. So it is with those who are faithful in distributing God's gifts. By imparting they increase their blessings. "Give, and it shall be given unto you," God has promised; "good measure, pressed down, and shaken

together, and running over, shall men give into your bosom." <u>Luke 6:38</u>."

— ACTS OF THE APOSTLES P. 345

Furthermore, it was Matthew Henry who said, "Note, Works of charity are so far from impoverishing us that they are the proper means truly to enrich us, or make us truly rich."[1] There are no better riches than an increase of faith. Therefore, we ought to take this counsel and look at it from multiple perspectives.

We too often look at the idea of giving as a financial matter, but the greatest gift you can give to God is yourself. "Commit your way to the Lord," the Psalmist wrote; Jesus Himself agrees with this notion, for He once disclosed regarding His own life: "I have power to lay it down, and I have power to take it again." The apostle Paul gave his best financial advice when he stated: "Owe no one anything except to love one another, for he who loves another has fulfilled the law." (Psalm 37:5; John 10:18; Romans 13:8). Apparently, there is something in us that God wants more than our pockets. As a Father, He pleads with His children

on this note, "My son, give me your heart, and let
your eyes observe my ways" (Proverbs 23:26).

Use me today as you see fit my Lord
To lift a sinner out of the pit of the
    world
To hearken to your word and stand
    still
Always obeying your will
To go, when you lead the way
To happily do so, when you want
    me to stay
Though I may sometimes come
    with empty pocket
Take my heart into your treasury
    and lock-it
This one thing I must learn
That the seed of love yields greater
    return
Help me rise to recognize
That at times I need to bend to
    bless
Sit to serve
And give to gain.

Dear Child of God, I plead with you. Don't
send your pocket to the front lines while keeping

your heart at base. The best is yet to be given when you give your last dollar. Give God your heart. How can I do this, you may ask? Well, allow me to turn the question back to you. What would Jesus do? He spent time with the outcast, and ate with sinners. He took interest in the cause of the poor and listened to their worries and woes.

We often say that a house is not a home. If you believe in this, then give the homeless a home in your heart and not a house in your town. He needs a friendly family not a fancy shelter. Spend time with them, listen with compassion, and be present — body, mind, and soul. Even one smile may push the handicap another mile, keep the dying alive for a while, and make the naked feel in style.

Lastly, make this practical for yourself. As long as the streets where we walk have beggars and prostitutes, drug addicts, and homeless people, there will be a mission field close to everyone. What can you do today to alleviate the suffering of humanity?

According to Matthew 25, when Jesus Christ comes the second time, He will offer unto us a harvest based on the nature of our sowing. With this in mind, there is much more I could say, but I just may allow Paul to conclude this essay.

"But this I say, He which soweth sparingly shall reap also sparingly; and he which soweth bountifully shall reap also bountifully. Every man according as he purposeth in his heart, so let him give; not grudgingly, or of necessity: for God loveth a cheerful giver. And God is able to make all grace abound toward you; that ye, always having all sufficiency in all things, may abound to every good work" (2 Corinthians 9:6-8).

---

1. "Commentary on 2 Corinthians 9 by Matthew Henry," Blue Letter Bible, accessed March 8, 2024, https://www. blueletterbible.org/Comm/mhc/2Cr/2Cr_009.cfm?a= 1087006.

8

BE PERSISTENT

When asking for favors from friends, family, or organizations, two social cues should be considered: the frequency of your request and the timing of when you ask. Let me explain. If you show up at a friend's house right after he has tucked his children into bed and commenced a sweet conversation with his beloved wife, let's say, between 9-10 PM, how do you think he would feel? Interrupted, perhaps? That's to say the least.

Consider another scenario: needing something and showing up at a friend's house every single day, seeking to persuade him into lending, giving, or helping you with something. How do you think he would feel? Probably not so fond of your behavior. Although he loves you, he is still a human with his own needs and responsibilities to care for, including those of his family. As much as he may be willing to help, he may not always be available.

The wisest of Israel, Solomon, a timeless sage, counseled his people to navigate social interactions carefully. He once stated, "Seldom set foot in your neighbor's house, lest he become weary of you and hate you" (Proverbs 25:17). This advice underscores the significance of being mindful of how frequently we approach others, even within the bonds of friendship. The acknowledgment that our friends, like ourselves, are human beings, should override the notion that we can ask for anything at any time.

On a similar note, have you ever paused to contemplate how we should relate to Jesus as a friend? In a significant moment, He told His disciples, "No longer do I call you servants, for a servant does not know what his master is doing; but I have called you friends, for all things that I heard from My Father I have made known to you" (John 15:15). The King who reigns supreme over every potentate and power chose to call us friends. Isn't that a beautiful and gentle gesture of love? I, too, believe it is—an amazing taste of bliss.

The question arises: how are we to relate to Jesus as our friend? Is our interaction limited to specific times and occurrences? I would respectfully differ with anyone answering yes to this question. As substantial proof to support my argument, I present the parable of the Unjust Judge that Jesus shared with those facing hardship and delay. In the following words lie valuable lessons for every human being.

> "1) Then He spoke a parable to them, that men always ought to pray and not lose heart, 2) saying: "There was in a certain city a judge who did not fear God nor regard man. 3) Now there was a widow in that city; and she came to him, saying, 'Get justice for me from my adversary.' 4) And he would not for a while; but afterward he said within himself, 'Though I do not fear God nor regard man, 5) yet because this widow troubles me I will avenge her, lest by her continual coming she weary me.'"
> 6) Then the Lord said, "Hear what the unjust judge said. 7) And shall God not avenge His own elect who cry out day and night to Him, though He bears long

with them? 8) I tell you that He will avenge them speedily. Nevertheless, when the Son of Man comes, will He really find faith on the earth?"

— LUKE 18-1-8

Through this parable, Jesus vividly taught that while earthly institutions and friends may, at times, turn us down, leading to despondency, we are to hold a different perspective when it comes to God. Even in His apparent delays, designed for our growth and the development of our faith, He always hears and answers our prayers.

For this reason, I believe, He said, "men always ought to pray and not lose heart" (verse 1). If even an unjust judge considers the case of one who perseveres, demonstrating the depth of his faith and the height of his courage, how much more will Jesus, the Just Judge, "avenge His own elect who cry out day and night to Him" (verse 7)?

Dear child of God, do not fail to show up in God's house continually, just as the widow did before the unjust judge. Extend the arms of solidarity and share the smiles of joy with those around you. Persevere through hardship and pray without ceasing. It doesn't matter if you can't see the growth yet, nor does it matter that you haven't received the desired answer yet. Hold on a little longer.

Sometimes, the tree of experience can only be brought to fruition when it's watered with tears of frustration. Don't give up. Christ isn't like our earthly friends; He knows no limit. However, at times, He waits a little before answering, giving us the opportunity to exercise the principle of "continual coming." Keep on coming; weeping may endure for a night, but when the dark cloud of gloom is folded away like a curtain, the sunshine of your joy will serve as a reminder that it is worth persevering even through the darkest nights. If you've failed to grasp the point of all this, remember: You may come to Christ at any time, for anything, as often as you desire. May the Lord be the Just Judge of your case.

9

LET GOD GUIDE YOU

As consistent as the river flows to the sea and waves roll to shore, so does the righteous enjoy peace. The story is told that once in his ministry, Jesus Christ was found sleeping in the frail old vessel of his poor disciples, in the middle of a raging storm.

Dear child of God, what is keeping you up at night? Embark on the journey of trusting and serving God, and let the Holy Spirit be the wind that guides your vessel. Do not succumb to the trials and tribulations of life. Live a life that, by default, is a testament to your faithfulness to God and an automatic disagreement with Satan's voice in your head.

When Satan murmurs his enticing voice in our

ears, we should quote God's promises back at him. Jesus' overcoming power that always pulled Him through the dark, tempting hours was found in the sentence: "It is written." When I am carnal, and my battle is spiritual, what I think matters little. Therefore, in times of trials, should rise to the height of my Savior's thoughts and quote it back at the enemy of mankind.

If you lose a loved one and Satan seeks to make you feel abandoned by God, resort to God's unfailing promises and tell him, "It is written: 'As I was with Moses, so I will be with you; I will never leave you nor forsake you'" (Joshua 1:5). When you experience financial hardship and find yourself buried in bills and trampled by trials, remember that it is also written: "Keep your lives free from the love of money and be content with what you have because God has said, "Never will I leave you; never will I forsake you" (Hebrews 13:5).

God's guidance shouldn't be sought only in the absence of trials but especially under trials. Let God guide you. His promises have proven faithful both theologically and historically. This is evidenced in the story of Horacio Spafford.

A renowned hymn writer and successful businessman in Chicago, Horacio Spafford, faced a sudden and devastating loss when all his properties were consumed by a mysterious fire in just a day. The impact on the Spafford family's finances must have been unimaginable.

Despite this tragedy, Horacio as a good father and a great husband, made a selfless decision. He sent his family, including his wife Anna and their four daughters, on a journey to England while he stayed back to manage the aftermath of the destruction of his dreams and real estate.

Several weeks later, Horacio received a heart-wrenching telegram that began with just two words: "Saved alone." The ship carrying his family had collided with another and sunk, taking the lives of their four daughters. Anna, however, miraculously survived. Facing such a profound tragedy, how would you respond?

Horacio abandoned all his immediate tasks and rushed to England. During his journey across the ocean, where the waters had claimed the lives of his beloved daughters, one can only imagine his tears increasing the volume of the Atlantic. Upon learning the exact location where his daughters had drowned, Horacio's response was immortalized in the form of poetry, now known worldwide as a household hymn. Out of his sorrowful heart, immersed in melancholy, Horacio penned these words:[1]

When peace like a river, attendeth
my way
When sorrows like sea billows roll
Whatever my lot, thou hast taught me
to say
It is well, it is well, with my soul

My sin, oh, the bliss of this glorious
thought!
My sin, not in part but the whole
Is nailed to the cross, and I bear it
no more
Praise the Lord, praise the Lord, o my
soul!

O Lord, haste the day when my faith
shall be sight,
the clouds be rolled back as a scroll;
the trump shall resound and the Lord
shall descend;
even so, it is well with my soul.

It is well with my soul;
it is well, it is well with my soul.

What an astounding response to trials. "When peace like a river, attendeth my way," he wrote.

This reminds us of that beautiful promise in the book of Isaiah, which states: "This is what the Lord says—your Redeemer, the Holy One of Israel: "I am the Lord your God, who teaches you what is best for you, who directs you in the way you should go. If only you had paid attention to my commands, your peace would have been like a river, your well-being like the waves of the sea" (Isaiah 48:17-18).

When your life is under trial, if you turn to God, your peace will be as sure as the river flows to the sea and as constant as the waves come to shore. Trust God and obey His word. Once more, in whatever you do, let God guide you.

———————————

1. "The Story behind the Hymn, What a Friend We Have in Jesus..Flv," www.youtube.com, January 27, 2012, https://youtu.be/tKjUoE2fack?feature=shared.

10

DO NOT ACCOMPLISH THINGS IN
A SINFUL WAY

"Rest in the Lord and wait patiently for Him." The most crucial principles for human existence often dripped from the lips of the psalmist in the form of poetry accompanied by the sweet sound of a well-tuned harp. This placed the sinner in harmony with the LORD and created a melody of joy in his heart. This is and must be the experience of the saved. He rejoices and rests in the LORD, not in the security afforded him by his bank account, not in the social recognition we often crave, and certainly not in the idea of doing better than others.

In fact, this call to rest found in Psalm 37, came attached to the idea of ceasing to scheme and cheat in order to succeed. A sincere Christian knows nothing but to wait patiently for the LORD. This he does when his turmoil is external and even more when it is internal. "Rest in the Lord, and wait patiently for Him; do not fret because of him who prospers in his way, because of the man who brings wicked schemes to pass" (Psalm 37:7).

Notice that David is speaking to those who were becoming unrestful through comparing themselves with the wicked man becoming "successful," while those who personally served the LORD were experiencing setbacks. Regardless, fret not, rest! The faith with which you cling to the rope of the LORD's strength determines whether you fall into the dark abyss of despondency or rise to the hill of holiness. If you hold tight to the promise of the LORD, you may reach the peak of peace.

Rest in the LORD! This is a solemn enjoinment or command, yet in the form of a promise. The same God who proclaimed the universe into existence with the simple phrase "Let there be..." is here saying: "Rest in the LORD..." Again, with the firm hands of faith you may hold on to this promise and find the rest that Jesus offers. Explicitly, He stated: "Come to Me, all you who labor and are heavy laden, and I will give you rest" (Matthew 11:28).

One author argues that this promise of rest extends far beyond mere inactivity. It is a spiritual phenomenon. We, therefore, must seek for it outside of and in spite of physical rest.

66 Jesus says, "Abide in Me." These words convey the idea of rest, stability, confidence. Again He invites, "Come unto Me, ... and I will give you rest." Matthew 11:28. The words of the psalmist express the same thought: "Rest in the Lord, and wait patiently for Him." And Isaiah gives the assurance, "In quietness and in confidence shall be your strength." Psalm 37:7; Isaiah 30:15. This rest is not found in inactivity; for in the Saviour's invitation the promise of rest is united with the call to labor: "Take My yoke upon you: ... and ye shall find rest." Matthew 11:29. The heart that rests most fully upon Christ will be most earnest and active in labor for Him.

— STEPS TO CHRIST P. 71

Dear child of God, I know you must have

plans. I know you must have dreams. However, the way to go about making these come true isn't at all by starting on the premise of comparisons between you and the successful evildoer, who wins his bread with the bitter sweat of cheating, scheming, violence, and an entire disregard for God's ways. As for you, my friend, take your lamb-like plan and lay it on the altar of service for God. Having done so, then you may "Commit your way to the Lord, Trust also in Him, And He shall bring it to pass" (Psalm 37:5). With such promise in mind, how can we not "Rest in the Lord, and wait patiently for Him?"

11

BE OBEDIENT TO AUTHORITIES

Emperor is the term we use today to depict those who served in the monarchial headship of the ancient Roman Empire. However, this term is an altogether modern convention and did not exist during the days of the Roman Empire. Within that period of history, an emperor was called a Caesar. While the ones who aren't so apt to embark on the study of history may think that Caesar was a name, it was actually a title given to many emperors.

Some scholars believe that Augustus, "also called Augustus Caesar, was the first Roman emperor following the republic, which had been finally destroyed by the dictatorship of Julius Caesar."1 He came to power at a point in history where patience and efficiency were like the golden mine of Ophir. This need he did not discard or overlook. "With unlimited patience, skill, and efficiency, he overhauled every aspect of Roman life and brought durable peace and prosperity to the Greco-Roman world."[1]

From one Caesar to another, passing the baton from one dictator to the next, such is the way the Roman Empire sought to perpetuate its power and dominate the earth. In the days when the tender maidens of the sons of man were used and abused, trodden and trampled, Jesus Christ came to this earth to establish his Kingdom of righteousness.

The Caesars of Rome rose to preeminence to the point of being called Dominus Noster (our Lord), but Jesus came as Sanctissimus Dominus Noster (our most Holy Lord). The Romans used swords to establish themselves as a kingdom and enact laws, but Jesus lowered the tip of His powerful scepter over the foundation of the word of God. He himself said it best when He declared: "My kingdom is not of this world. If My kingdom were of this world, My servants would fight, so that I should not be delivered to the Jews; but now My kingdom is not from here" (John 18:36).

Now, here comes the golden question - should the follower of Jesus Christ disobey the modern

Caesars of this world because Jesus is Sanctissimus Dominus Noster? Here is what the Apostle Paul had to say on the matter: "Let every soul be subject to the governing authorities. For there is no authority except from God, and the authorities that exist are appointed by God" (Romans 13:1). Further along in this same chapter, he added, "For because of this you also pay taxes, for they are God's ministers attending continually to this very thing. Render therefore to all their due: taxes to whom taxes are due, customs to whom customs, fear to whom fear, honor to whom honor" (verses 6, 7).

Jesus Christ, Sanctissimus Dominus Noster, dominates the world of politicians and is able to move the hands that move the gavel in our court system. While we may make laws and establish statutes on earth, Jesus still serves as Dominus Litis (He has dominion over the case). He can rule and overrule and lead His people to their desired haven even amidst the chaos of our law-making bodies. Be at ease. What we are presenting to you here isn't anecdotal — it has been tested and tried throughout the course of history and proven to be nothing short of infallible.

Notice this. In the book of Micah, God gave a Messianic prophecy that indicated the exact location where Jesus would be born. "But you, Bethlehem Ephrathah," the prophet wrote, "Though you are little among the thousands of Judah, yet out of you shall come forth to Me The One to be Ruler in Israel, Whose goings forth are from of old, from everlasting" (Micah 5:2). There is a wide consensus amongst scholars and theologians that this is a prophecy of the birth of Jesus, apart from the fact the Bible itself leaves this without a doubt. However, how did this prophecy regarding the location of Jesus' birth fulfill?

According to the reckoning of Luke, Joseph left Galilee when "a decree went out from Caesar Augustus that all the world should be registered. This census first took place while Quirinius was governing Syria. So all went to be registered, everyone to his own city" (Luke 2:1-3). Furthermore, he specified the destination and the purpose of Joseph and Mary's journey on the following verses.

"Joseph also went up from Galilee, out of the city of Nazareth, into Judea, to the city of David, which is called Bethlehem, because he was of the house and lineage of David, to be registered with Mary, his betrothed wife, who was with child. So it was, that while they were there, the days were completed for her to be delivered. And she brought forth her firstborn Son, and wrapped Him in swaddling cloths, and laid Him in a manger, because there was no room for them in the inn" (Luke 2:4-7).

Alleluia! Glory to the LORD! Sanctissimus Dominus Noster is Jesus Christ. The word of God had said that He would be born in the City of David, no matter the circumstances. When Caesar Augustus enacted the laws that sent every citizen to their hometown for census participation, it was but a political matter. Nonetheless, behind the curtains of the dramatic political history stood the gigantic personage of the LORD our God raising His canvass to the height of the sky while painting His providence for all who care to see.

WOW! You may, dear child of GOD, trust His words and follow His providences. When we obey the government as Christians, we are acknowledging that God's hands are behind the curtain working out something better for us. As far as we can with a clean conscience be subject to authorities, we may be so in the hope that Christ will guide us through the debris of this fragmented world. Little does it matter which president is chosen next. Little does it matter what tax and tribute we have to pay. If we stand with Jesus Christ, we will obey the authorities as long as they don't lead us against the word of God.

Lastly, the notion of disobeying authorities is not to be confused with the need to fight for that which is right. Daniel fought for the right in Babylon, even against the will of King Nebuchadnezzar. Joseph and Moses both fought for the right in Egypt in the sight of the world's greatest tyrants, the Pharaohs. Therefore, when you are called to fight for right even in the face of governmental opposition, stand on the word of God, and do so humbly. Additionally, we must move forward knowing that there isn't any biblical augment in favor of rebellion in the case of honoring the authorities, paying our taxes and responding to the voice our court systems when we are summoned.

As you obey the laws of the land that does not contradict with the word of God, do so in peace and assurance that God's hands are behind the curtains guiding the affairs of our world and fulfilling His eternal and holy desire. Above all, remember, Jesus is Sanctissimus Dominus Noster.

---

1. "Who Was the First Roman Emperor? | Britannica,"

www.britannica.com, n.d., https://www.britannica.com/question/Who-was-the-first-Roman-emperor.

CONTACT INFORMATION

Have you been blessed by this book?

Please share your feedback with us:

Email: angelobarb@aol.com

Phone: 718 622 4821

Office Address: 535 Dean st. Suite 121 Brooklyn NY, 11217

ACKNOWLEDGMENTS

Formatting and Editing:
Deivon de Andrade (860-367-2689)
Imani Charles (860-367-2689)

Cover Design:
Kevin Burton

Proofreading:
Sandy Holdson